4/14

YOU CHOOSE
BOOKS™

THE MAKING OF THE
SOCIAL
NETWORK

AN INTERACTIVE MODERN HISTORY ADVENTURE

by Michael Burgan

Consultant:
Alan Winegarden, PhD
Chair, Department of Communication Studies
Concordia University, St. Paul, Minnesota

CAPSTONE PRESS
a capstone imprint

You Choose Books are published by Capstone Press,
1710 Roe Crest Drive, North Mankato, Minnesota 56003
www.capstonepub.com

Library of Congress Cataloging-in-Publication Data
Burgan, Michael.
The making of the social network : an interactive modern history adventure / by
Michael Burgan.
pages cm. — (You choose books. You choose: modern)
Includes bibliographical references and index.
ISBN 978-1-4765-4188-4 (library binding)
ISBN 978-1-4765-5219-4 (paperback)
ISBN 978-1-4765-6065-6 (eBook PDF)
1. Online social networks—History—Juvenile literature. 2. Internet—Social aspects—
Juvenile literature. 3. Social media—History—Juvenile literature. I. Title.
HM742.B87 2014
302.23'1—dc23   2013036662

Editorial Credits
Michelle Hasselius and Angie Kaelberer, editors; Gene Bentdahl, designer;
Wanda Winch, media researcher; Danielle Ceminsky, production specialist

Photo Credits
AP Images/Associated Press Television, 103, Manuel Balce Ceneta, 55, Mario Jose
Sanchez, 52, Patrick Semansky, 42; Corbis: Reuters/Hyungwon Kang, 64, Will &
Deni McIntyre, 92; Courtesy of the National Security Agency, 66; Dreamstime: Kobby
Dagan, 37, Marcin Winnicki, 39; Getty Images Inc: Bloomberg/George Frey, 70;
iStockphoto Inc: ericsphotography, 35, GiorgioMagini, 32; Newscom: Getty Images
Inc/AFP/*The Guardian*, 60; PhotoEdit Inc: Christina Kennedy, 87, John Neubauer,
97, Michael Newman, 77; Shutterstock: Alexander Ermolaev, 100, alphaspirit, 16, 29,
Andre Viegas, paper background, Angela Waye, 49, bikeriderlondon, 27, catwalker,
11, chanpipat, 105, craig hill, 57, Dan Howell, 45, Goodluz, 24, grafvision, 6, Hurst
Photo, 74, Kamira, 99, oliveromg, 81, Peter Gudella, 21, Phase4Photography, 19,
phyZick, digital design background, Rafael Olechowski, 47, Sergey Nivens, cover, Syda
Productions, 80, YanLev, 83; U.S. Air Force, Courtesy of Harry S. Truman Library, 9

Printed in the United States of America in Stevens Point, Wisconsin.
092013   007765WZS14

TABLE OF CONTENTS

4

ABOUT YOUR
ADVENTURE

Just a few years ago, no one had heard of the social network. Now it seems as if everyone is using it to keep in touch with others, make new friends, and express their thoughts and opinions. But it can be misused as well.

In this book you'll explore how the choices people make can affect their lives and those of others. The events you'll experience happened to real people.

Chapter One sets the scene. Then you choose which path to read. Follow the directions at the bottom of each page. The choices you make will change your outcome. After you finish your path, go back and read the others for new perspectives and more adventures.

YOU CHOOSE the path
you take through history.

Social media helps people connect with each other all over the world.

The World of Social Media

You are living in the beginning of the 21st century, when computers link the world like never before. Social media is a common way to connect to friends and even to strangers. Using social media, you easily share information, pictures, and video on cell phones and computers.

The system that lets you use social media relies on the Internet. During the 1950s the U.S. government wanted new forms of technology for its military. It created the Defense Advanced Research Projects Agency (DARPA). In its first years it was known as ARPA.

7

Turn the page.

During the 1960s ARPA scientists explored the idea of linking computers at universities in various parts of the country. That way researchers could more easily share information.

Four schools—the University of California at Los Angeles, the University of Utah, Stanford University, and the University of California at Santa Barbara—were linked by phone lines in 1969, creating a network called ARPANET. Two years later ARPANET users began sending and receiving e-mails for the first time.

Through the 1970s new computer networks were built and connected, creating the Internet. The speed at which data flowed over the Internet increased, thanks to glass wires known as fiber optics.

President Truman signed the National Security Act in 1947, paving the way for the creation of DARPA.

The development of the personal computer in the mid-1970s was also a huge part of the Internet's growth. By the early 1980s IBM, Apple, and several other companies produced PCs. The personal computers were small and inexpensive enough for people to have them in their homes.

Swiss software designer Tim Berners-Lee created the World Wide Web in 1989. Using a computer language known as Hyper Text Markup Language (HTML), people could create pages of information and link them. They viewed the pages on computers using software applications called web browsers.

A 2000 postage stamp honored Tim Berners-Lee and his creation of the World Wide Web.

Berners-Lee created the first web browser, Nexus, in 1990. Three years later the National Center for Supercomputing Applications released Mosaic, which showed both text and images on web pages. Other browsers were later developed, including Netscape Navigator, Internet Explorer, Safari, and Mozilla Firefox.

By 1995 about 16 million people used the Web worldwide, many from their home computers. Ten years later the number had grown to more than 1 billion.

11

Some websites allowed computer users to directly communicate with each other. The users created profiles, which described who they were and what they liked. The users hoped to find people with similar interests. They also connected to people they already knew. These sites were the first examples of social media. Friendster was one of the early successes. It was launched in 2002.

Over the next 10 years, new social media appeared and grew quickly. Facebook became the largest social media company, with more than 1 billion users around the world. Many companies turned to social media to promote their services and products. Today even the U.S. president and other elected officials use social media to connect with voters.

You've used social media most of your life. But as you know, sometimes technology can be used in negative ways. As you get more involved in the world of social media, you'll face many decisions.

13

To be a college student creating a new social media site, turn to page **15.**

To be a government employee who keeps track of how social media is used, turn to page **43.**

To join a school club using social media to inform others about its cause, turn to page **75.**

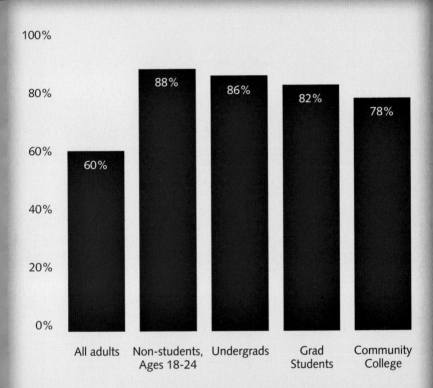

COLLEGE STUDENTS AND SOCIAL NETWORKING SITES

Percentage of Internet users in each group
who used social networking sites in 2010

100%	
80%	88% 86% 82% 78%
60%	60%
40%	
20%	
0%	

All adults | Non-students, Ages 18-24 | Undergrads | Grad Students | Community College

Source: Pew Research Center's Internet & American Life Project 2010 tracking surveys

CHAPTER 2

From College Kid to Internet Tycoon

It's early in the 2000s and you're heading to college. You've used computers since kindergarten and now write your own apps. When you get to the university, you want to use your computer skills to help students connect.

You develop an Internet site called SchoolBuddies. You list all the classes offered by the university. If users click on a class, they see which students are enrolled in it. If they click on friends' names, they see the classes they're taking. The other students love SchoolBuddies, since they can easily see if their friends are taking a certain class.

15

Turn the page.

With the success of SchoolBuddies, you meet other people interested in writing new Internet programs. One of them is Scott, a computer science student from California.

"I have an idea," Scott says. "Most of the kids like to use instant messaging. We could have them put up a list of the people they IM most often. Their friends could do it too. It would make it easier for groups of friends to get to know each other and share their interests."

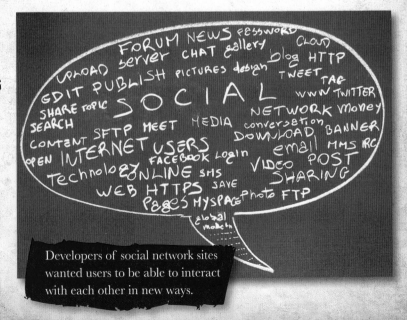

Developers of social network sites wanted users to be able to interact with each other in new ways.

"Maybe," you say. But you're already thinking about another idea of your own. Your university is divided into separate colleges. Each college has a book with pictures and information about its students. You want to help everyone in the various colleges see all the pictures and learn about the other students. You have the perfect name for your site—PictureBook.

"Do you want to help me?" Scott asks. "I want to call my site InstantFriends."

You like Scott, but you think your Internet idea is better. It might be good to work alone.

17

To work alone on your project, turn to page **18.**
To help Scott, turn to page **23.**

"That sounds like a great idea," you say. "But I've got some ideas of my own I want to develop."

"Well, OK," Scott says. He seems upset, but you think you've made the right decision.

You work on PictureBook every evening. To make it more interesting, you want students to be able to rate the pictures, picking out the best-looking girls and guys. Writing the computer code to create the program is easy. The hard part will be getting all the pictures from the various colleges' books. You have to be in a particular college to have access to the books.

You explain your idea to your roommate, Shannon. She offers to help.

"I know students in some of the colleges," she says. "I'll have them give me their passwords and get into their colleges' networks."

"Great!" you say. As Shannon leaves, you do some hacking and get into several networks on your own. Bugs in the software let you enter the systems without a password.

Many students use laptops in their college classes.

Turn the page.

Within a few days you have access to all the photos from 11 of the 12 colleges at the university. But you can't hack into the last network, which is Trumbull College. Shannon can't find anyone there who will share a password.

"You can always start PictureBook anyway," Shannon says. "You can get Trumbull later."

"No, I want them all on there right away," you reply. "I might have to sneak into Trumbull."

"You could get in trouble," Shannon warns.

20 She's right. But you hate the idea of not finishing what you start.

To sneak into Trumbull, go to page **21**.

To start PictureBook now, turn to page **34**.

Students are given their own user names and create passwords to use their college's Internet server.

You head over to Trumbull and watch as some students press the numbers that open the lock on the building's door. In a few minutes, you have the code and enter the building. Then you look for a study room and find an Ethernet plug. You plug in your laptop and access Trumbull's network. It takes you about 30 minutes to download the photos. You rush back to your room and add the new photos to PictureBook.

Turn the page.

Over the next few days, Shannon and some other friends check out the site. They like it, and they begin telling their friends about it. But several weeks go by, and not many people are joining PictureBook. Instead, everyone's talking about another new site—InstantFriends!

Scott has finished his program, and he's changed it. Like you, he's added pictures of all the students to his site.

You see Scott one afternoon coming out of class.

"You stole my idea," you say angrily.

"No," he says, smiling. "I just made my idea better. But I could use a good programmer. You can still work with me if you want."

You're upset with Scott for taking your idea. But if you work with him, you can make InstantFriends even better.

To work with Scott, turn to page **31**.

To keep working on PictureBook, turn to page **33**.

"OK, Scott, let's work together," you say.

Doing the programming for InstantFriends is easy, but you feel you can do more. You tell Scott about PictureBook.

"I like that," Scott says. "And I have another friend who's interested in social media too. Maybe we can work together."

Scott introduces you to Abby. She wants to set up a site where students can learn about events around town and arrange to go together. Companies might even pay to advertise on the site.

"I can get some money from my parents," Abby says. "But I don't know enough about programming to build the site."

Turn the page.

Social network sites are public, so users need to be careful what they share online.

You work with Abby and Scott to start the new site. It combines your idea to connect students at school with Abby's idea about promoting events. You name it ConnectBook.

24   After working for several weeks, you launch ConnectBook. Students across the university begin using it. They have to use their own names and take responsibility for what they post. But you let users keep some information private, such as their birthdates and home addresses.

Within weeks several thousand students are using ConnectBook. They tell their friends at other universities. You link those schools into the network. ConnectBook is a big hit.

"My dad wants to give us more money so we can expand beyond schools," Abby says.

"I'm not sure we're ready to grow that fast," Scott says. He looks at you. "What do you think?"

To go slowly, turn to page **26.**
To expand ConnectBook now, turn to page **29.**

"I agree with Scott," you say. "We should go slowly and make sure we do everything right."

Abby's father, Dan, agrees to let you run ConnectBook as you want. You add more features, such as giving each user a "wall." The people they're connected to can write messages on the wall, which other people can also see. And you set up groups that allow people with shared interests to connect.

As ConnectBook grows you realize that running the site is a full-time job. You and Scott leave school to focus on the business. Abby stays in college but is still a part owner. In less than a year after the launch, the network has 1 million users. Investors like it too.

Various companies offer you millions of dollars to buy ConnectBook. But you and Scott say no. You're ready to expand beyond colleges, and you want to be in control.

You buy more equipment and hire more employees. ConnectBook is a real company now, but not like the ones your parents work at. You have few rules. People come in late and wear casual clothes. But they work hard, sometimes spending all night in the small office you rent.

Social networking sites are not just geared for students. Many businesses see the value of social media to reach consumers.

Turn the page.

You build the company by expanding to more colleges and then to high schools. You accept more ads. And then you're ready to let anyone, not just students, register as a user.

Even more people want to buy ConnectBook—including major news and TV companies! Scott tells you that maybe you should listen to the offers.

"Look at this one," he says. "MediaBiz is offering us more than $500 million to buy ConnectBook!"

Your heart pounds a little—$500 million! Maybe you should sell. But if you keep ConnectBook, it could be worth even more some day.

28

To sell the company, turn to page **39**.

To keep it, turn to page **41**.

"We should take the money," you say.

Scott decides that he doesn't have time to work on a bigger ConnectBook. But he invests some money in the project.

With the money from Abby's father, Dan, you expand ConnectBook. You also make money selling ads to companies. The number of users at colleges continues to grow. Within months you have 100,000 users across the country. But you think you can get millions.

Many of today's businesses use marketing strategies that include social media.

Turn the page.

Over the next few months, you decide to leave college to focus on building ConnectBook.

One day you receive a letter from a lawyer's office. Scott is taking you and Abby to court! He says many of the ideas for ConnectBook were his. He wants more of the money you make.

"What should we do?" Abby asks.

"We can either fight Scott in court, or try to reach a settlement with him outside of court," you sigh.

You don't like the idea of a settlement. So much of the programming and basic ideas for ConnectBook were yours! But Scott did invest some time and money in the company. And a court case could get expensive.

To settle, turn to page **36.**

To go to court, turn to page **38.**

"All right," you say. ""But I want a contract to make sure I get paid if you make money from InstantFriends."

Scott agrees. You improve the code so it's easier for people to use InstantFriends. Scott decides to expand the service to other universities. You spend money to rent space on more servers. You keep working on the programming. Meanwhile, you're still taking classes. Some nights you're lucky if you get two or three hours of sleep.

All that hard work is worth it, though. Within six months InstantFriends has thousands of users across the country.

31

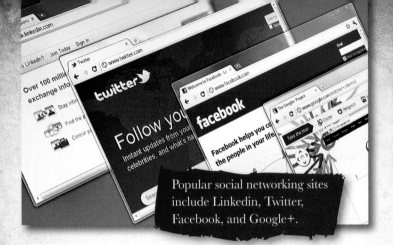

Popular social networking sites include Linkedin, Twitter, Facebook, and Google+.

You and Scott go to New York to meet with investors interested in the site. One investor, Craig Sanchez, offers $10 million to buy InstantFriends.

"Take it!" you whisper to Scott.

Scott nods and shakes Sanchez's hand. With the deal you made with Scott, you're going to be a millionaire! And you'll have plenty of time and money to come up with a new social media company of your own.

THE END

To follow another path, turn to page 11.
To read the conclusion, turn to page 101.

"Forget it," you tell Scott. "I can make it on my own."

Social media programs are becoming more popular everywhere. You can get friends you have at other universities to help you spread PictureBook.

On your spring break, you travel to some of the other universities. You decide to launch PictureBook at Harvard. There's just one problem—a social media site there is already very popular. A student named Mark Zuckerberg created something called Thefacebook. It's almost exactly like PictureBook! And he's already spread his site to other schools.

33

Sadly, you decide to give up on PictureBook. Social media networks are here to stay, but yours just wasn't the right one.

THE END

To follow another path, turn to page 11.
To read the conclusion, turn to page 101.

"It's not worth getting in trouble," you tell Shannon. "When everyone sees how great PictureBook is, the students at Trumbull will want to be on too."

You launch PictureBook later that week. Sure enough, someone at Trumbull gives you his password so you can get the college's photos. But before you put the pictures on the site, you get a call from Dean Rita Werner at the university. She wants to see you in her office. When you get there, several young women are with the dean.

The dean says, "These students come from
a women's group on campus. They aren't happy about some of the comments the male students are leaving about the girls."

"I don't limit what people post," you say.

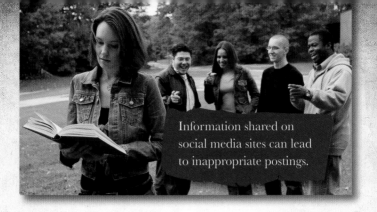
Information shared on social media sites can lead to inappropriate postings.

"Did you have permission to use these pictures?" Dean Werner asks. "Or permission to use the university's computer network?"

"No, Ms. Werner."

She tells you to shut down the service. "And I think you should use your talents for something useful," the dean says. "I want you to build websites for the group these women represent."

You nod. Someday you'll start another social media site—but maybe after you finish college.

THE END

To follow another path, turn to page 11.
To read the conclusion, turn to page 101.

"We don't have the money for a legal battle," you tell Abby.

Abby agrees. Her father contacts a lawyer. You agree to give Scott 5 percent ownership in ConnectBook. By now the company is growing faster than ever.

"That 5 percent will make Scott rich someday," Abby says.

"But we'll be even richer," you reply.

ConnectBook makes the news as it grows. Word of your settlement with Scott spreads too. One day Abby comes into your office holding a letter.

"It's another lawsuit!" she wails.

Mark Zuckerberg became a billionaire after creating Facebook. He was involved in legal disputes with people who claimed they helped develop his site.

Abby explains that when she was thinking about starting a social network, she discussed the idea with her friends. Now some claim they helped her create ConnectBook.

"What should we do?" she asks.

"This time we're fighting," you say.

You know ConnectBook is a good idea. But you wish you had more time to improve it, rather than worrying about court battles.

THE END

To follow another path, turn to page 11.
To read the conclusion, turn to page 101.

"Scott should only get what he deserves based on what he invested," you say. "Let's get a lawyer."

Abby agrees. A long court battle begins. ConnectBook continues to grow. Scott is determined to keep the legal fight going. Three years later he agrees to accept stock in the company and several million dollars in cash.

Abby tells you that she's heard Scott plans to invest in more social network companies.

"Good for him," you say. "We have hundreds of millions of users around the world—and we're still growing. He'll never be as successful as ConnectBook."

THE END

To follow another path, turn to page 11.
To read the conclusion, turn to page 101.

"Maybe it is time to sell," you say. "Let's talk to Abby and see what she says."

Abby agrees you should sell. Dan helps you make the deal with MediaBiz. When it's done you walk away with more than $100 million!

You decide you'll use the money to start another social media site—one to share photos easily. As you start working, you read about your old company. ConnectBook is losing customers to Facebook, another social media site.

According to Facebook, the social media site reached 1 billion members in 2012.

Turn the page.

As Facebook and other new social media sites grow, fewer companies advertise on ConnectBook. As time goes on you hear that ConnectBook is struggling to survive. Finally MediaBiz sells it at a huge loss.

You're sad to see the idea you helped create go through such tough times. But you know that some companies do well at first and keep growing. Others die. You just hope your new company doesn't end up like ConnectBook.

THE END

To follow another path, turn to page 11.
To read the conclusion, turn to page 101.

"ConnectBook is worth more than what MediaBiz wants to pay," you say. "And I know we can keep the company growing."

Scott trusts you. With each year the number of ConnectBook users grows, even as new social media sites appear. The value of your share of the company increases. After a few years you decide to make some money off ConnectBook. But instead of selling it to a big company, you decide to sell stock in the company to investors who want to pay the price. Your shares are worth several billion dollars.

You decide to sell some shares and step away from the company. You want to spend time with your family. You have plenty of shares left, and you'll still have a role to play at ConnectBook.

THE END

To follow another path, turn to page 11.
To read the conclusion, turn to page 101.

41

The National Security Agency in
Fort Meade, Maryland.

CHAPTER 3

Spying and Social Media

You work for the National Security
Agency. The NSA collects what is called signal
intelligence—phone calls and digital messages
sent from around the world. NSA workers then
go through the information to see if they can
learn about foreign threats to American security.
The agency also works to make sure enemies can't
attack the U.S. government's computer networks
and communication systems.

43

Turn the page.

You and others at the NSA work with secret information. Getting a job here took almost a year. You had to go through medical tests and a lie-detector test. The agency also questioned your family and friends to make sure you would be loyal.

You started your career at the NSA headquarters in Fort Meade, Maryland. But now you're being offered a transfer to the new Utah Data Center. The center will store information such as what people put in their e-mails or online searches. NSA analysts will also find and review information sent by users over networks protected by passwords. The NSA has made huge gains in breaking the encryption that's supposed to keep digital information private.

In Utah you'll analyze data that comes in from around the world—and even from the United States. After the September 11, 2001, terrorist attacks, the government began recording phone conversations and checking e-mails of some Americans, even if they weren't suspected of planning a crime. In 2008 Congress said it was legal for the NSA to do this under certain conditions. The goal was to prevent another terrorist attack in the United States.

The September 11, 2001, terrorist attacks prompted tighter security measures.

Turn the page.

You think the job in Utah could be interesting. But your boss, Joe, also offers you a new job here in Maryland.

"We're worried about new cyberwarfare attacks on our computer systems," he says. "Some attacks could destroy the country's communications. Even hacking of social media can cause problems. Remember that post about the White House?"

You remember. It happened in April 2013. Someone hacked the Twitter account of a major news agency. The post said that terrorists had attacked the White House. Some people who read the fake message panicked. Criminals also have hacked into social media companies' servers and stolen clients' credit card information.

To stay in Maryland, go to page **47**.

To go to the Utah Data Center, turn to page **51**.

"I'll stay here and help fight cyberwarfare," you tell Joe.

Though you took computer science classes all through college, you never learned how to break into secure computer networks. Other NSA analysts and engineers teach you the basics of hacking. You learn about getting access to websites that have poor security. You can also send people e-mail attachments that include special code you write. If the receiver opens the attachment, the code changes a program on the receiver's computer. This gives you a "backdoor" to retrieve information.

47

Terms related to Internet hacking keep multiplying.

Turn the page.

You learn more about the dangers of foreign attacks on U.S. computer systems. Some steal information from U.S. companies. Others send viruses to infect computers so they can't function properly.

"A lot of the attacks come from Asia," Joe explains. "And someday a foreign country could attack our military computers as part of a war."

You become skilled at using the techniques to break into computer networks and individual computers. Joe asks if you'd like to specialize.

"We need network defense—that is, to try to stop incoming attacks," Joe says. "But we need offense too. We might need to attack another country's networks before they attack ours."

To pursue cyberwar offense, go to page **49**.
To pursue cyberwar defense, turn to page **63**.

Many computer icons are used to alert people of potential viruses.

"If we need to attack another country to defend the United States, I'm ready to help," you say.

Your training continues. But instead of learning only how to break into a computer network, you look for ways to destroy one. Joe tells you that he wants you to help build a worm. Unlike a virus, a worm spreads from one computer to another without users downloading any kind of file.

49

Turn the page.

The harmful code spreads on its own between computers in networks that run a certain kind of software. The code can also be spread when an infected storage device is put into a computer.

"Are we going to use the worm to attack a foreign country?" you ask.

"I don't know," Joe says. "This is a top-secret project. But I also have another important project you could work on."

Joe explains that the government wants to do a simulation of a cyber attack. Computer simulations help the military learn about what could happen on the battlefield under certain conditions. A cyber attack simulation might try to predict what would happen if enemy computers attacked U.S. military or business computers.

To work on the worm, turn to page **61**.
To work on the simulation, turn to page **65**.

50

Joe shakes your hand and wishes you luck. You find an apartment in Bluffdale, Utah, site of the new data center.

Your new boss, Mary, takes you around the center. It includes several buildings. "We have our own generators for electricity," Mary says. "And we can purify our own water." She also tells you about the information you'll be collecting. "If someone does an Internet search or sends an e-mail, we can collect the information and store it here."

"Even if someone hasn't done anything wrong?" you ask.

"That's right. We need all the data we can get before something bad happens. Besides, everyone should know that what people post on the Internet isn't really private. Even if they delete it from the computer, it's still on the Web."

Turn the page.

You know that it's legal for the government to secretly collect information about Americans who are overseas. But you didn't realize it also collects information on some Americans who may not be suspected terrorists. Mary explains that the NSA has software that helps protect people's privacy. You hope it works.

A few weeks later you talk to another analyst, Miguel. "I want to fight terrorism," you tell him. "But I don't like the government secretly accessing what people do online."

The social media site, Twitter, was hacked in January 2013. It affected 250,000 users.

"I guess if you haven't done anything wrong, you don't have anything to worry about," Miguel says. He explains that the NSA had another software program that could collect data and protect privacy better than the one it currently uses. But NSA officials decided to use the current system instead. You ask why, but Miguel doesn't know.

"Maybe someone should tell the media about what's going on," you say. "Or other people in government."

"If you do, you could get fired," Miguel says.

To tell someone about the better software program, turn to page **54.**

To keep quiet, turn to page **72.**

You need to tell someone about the two software programs. The country should use the best possible system to collect data and protect privacy. But you don't tell Miguel about your decision. You don't want to get him in trouble.

The other software program is called CatchPhrase. Not only was it better than the current program, it was also cheaper to create and use. You ask some people about CatchPhrase, but no one wants to talk about it.

One night you get a phone call at home.

"I hear you want to know about CatchPhrase," a man on the other end says.

"Who are you?" you ask.

"Just call me Bob. I used to work at the NSA."

General Keith Alexander, head of the U.S. Cyber Command and NSA, has testified about cyberspace operations.

Bob explains that in the days after the September 11 attacks, the NSA listened to phone calls that some Americans made. The NSA did this without warrants, which police and the FBI need to listen to private calls. The NSA collected and read private e-mails too.

55

"The government was breaking the law," Bob said. "I tried to tell people in government, but no one would listen. So I quit and became a whistle-blower. I told the media what I knew about what the government was doing."

Turn the page.

Bob says he wants to give the media more information about any possible illegal NSA activities. "Will you help me?" he asks.

You believe what Bob says. But you worry that helping him will get you into trouble.

To work with Bob, go to page **57**.

To say no, turn to page **68**.

"I'll do it," you say. "As long as I don't have to break the law."

Bob explains that he works with a blogger in Washington, D.C. The blog, It's True, publishes information about the government.

"If you can find any information about what's going on in the Data Center, she'd like to see it."

"I won't give her anything that's classified," you say.

"She understands that," Bob says. "Give the information to me, and I'll get it to her."

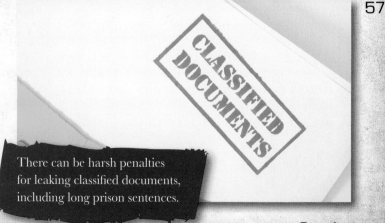

There can be harsh penalties for leaking classified documents, including long prison sentences.

Turn the page.

Your palms start to sweat. Bob isn't a criminal, but your bosses wouldn't want you helping him. But you know whistle-blowers like Bob help Americans learn the truth about what their government does.

"We shouldn't talk on the phone anymore," you say.

You tell Bob to set up a fake account on Facebook and then send you a friend request. You set up a code to arrange when you can meet in person.

Over the next few weeks, you look into various programs on the NSA computers. You find some unclassified information and give it to Bob. The next week he sends you a message: "Check out today's It's True post." The blogger has used your information.

You are pleased, but you worry that you could be linked to the story, even though your name isn't mentioned.

That night there's a knock on your door. You open it and see several men holding guns. "FBI," one of them says. "We have a warrant to search your house." They go through your belongings and take your computer. They don't arrest you, but you know you need a lawyer.

Someone has connected you with Bob and the blogger. You go to work the next day, but Mary tells you to take some time off. "What happened at your house last night doesn't look good," she says.

You meet with Carla Smith, a lawyer Bob recommended. She says the government is charging you with espionage.

Turn the page.

"Espionage!" you say. "I didn't spy on anyone, or work with a foreign government!"

"The charges say you were spreading secret information," Carla says. "You can try to make a deal, so they give you a lighter punishment. Or you can go to trial. If you're convicted, you could face 20 years in jail."

You could lose in a court trial. But making a deal means you're admitting you're guilty—and you aren't.

Edward Snowden, an employee of the NSA, leaked top-secret files to the newspaper, *The Guardian*, in 2013.

To make a deal, turn to page **69**.

To go to trial, turn to page **70**.

You join a team of computer experts working on the worm. Cyber experts from Israel are taking part too. Your goal is to disrupt the machines enemies use to make nuclear weapons not allowed by international peace agreements.

Your leader on the project, Denise, explains what will happen with the worm.

"As you know, uranium is used in nuclear bombs. For the bomb to work, the uranium has to go through a process called enrichment.

"Our job is to get into the computers that control the machines that enrich the uranium. The worm will make the machines break down."

61

It takes your team several weeks to write the code that will create the worm, which is nicknamed Starnet.

Turn the page.

Once the worm gets into an enemy computer, it will make more copies of itself and spread to other machines. Then it will look for the computers that have the software you want to target. That software controls the enriching machines.

Finally the day comes to release Starnet. Months pass. One day you get good news. Something has damaged the machines at the enemy country's uranium-enrichment plant. The worm worked! You and the rest of your team celebrate. But you know enemy countries will continue to try to illegally make nuclear weapons. People like you will have to keep fighting cyberwarfare to protect the United States and its allies.

62

THE END

To follow another path, turn to page 11.
To read the conclusion, turn to page 101.

You are assigned to a team of NSA experts who are helping rebel fighters in the Middle East. The U.S. government doesn't want to get directly involved in the fighting, but it wants the rebels to win. Your new boss, Henry, explains the situation.

"The rebels rely on social media to post messages to their supporters," he says. "But their government is attacking their accounts. The government also attacks the accounts of journalists who are covering the war. The government says the journalists spread lies."

Creating defense for cyber attacks isn't easy. The Internet isn't under the control of any one government. Many of the networks are privately owned.

63

Turn the page.

The National Cybersecurity and Communications Integration Center in Arlington, Virginia, is also involved in protecting the U.S. in cyberspace.

Your team is working with network experts from social media companies. Your goal is to protect the social media accounts of the rebels and the journalists who write about them.

You spend your days in front of a computer screen. After several weeks you hack into the foreign government's computer system. You shut down the government's network. The rebels can send their messages again. You're glad you were able to help them.

THE END

To follow another path, turn to page 11.
To read the conclusion, turn to page 101.

Joe explains that the government wants its workers and business leaders to explore what could happen during a real cyberwar.

"We're going to base the simulation on some real events," he explains. "Just a few years ago, hackers in Iran tried to shut down business computers here in the United States. The hackers had ties to the Iranian government. And since Iran and the United States don't have good relations, cyber attacks could lead to real trouble."

You and several other programmers work on a simulation game for several weeks. In the game you help invent, Iran's government orders attacks against U.S. websites and social media companies. The companies want to fight back with their own cyber attacks, but the U.S. government wants to control the situation.

65

Turn the page.

"That's a good storyline," Joe tells you. "The companies want to protect themselves because the U.S. government doesn't control the networks. U.S. government leaders believe they need to control the response to the attacks."

"But what about us attacking another country with computers?" you ask him. "Can I work on a simulation like that?"

Joe agrees, and you design a new simulation. In it the United States launches a cyber attack on Iran.

Simulations help government organizations prepare for real-life cyber attacks against the U.S.

The Iranians respond with their own attacks and bring in other groups to help. The hackers shut down the computers that control the U.S. electrical system. You have the president respond by launching real missiles against Iran. The two countries go to war.

Joe looks over the simulation. "That's not a happy game," he says somberly.

"I know. But it could happen."

Joe nods. You both hope a cyberwar never leads to a real one.

67

THE END

To follow another path, turn to page 11.
To read the conclusion, turn to page 101.

"No," you say. "I don't want to lose my job."

"All right," Bob says. "But let me know if you change your mind."

That night you research NSA whistle-blowers. You learn someone who could be Bob worked on CatchPhrase, but he left the government years ago. He learned that the NSA was using a version of CatchPhrase that didn't protect Americans' privacy. After he left the NSA, Bob spoke out against the illegal access of phone conversations and e-mails.

You don't believe Bob has done anything illegal. But you're already more involved than you'd like to be. You decide to stop worrying about CatchPhrase. You like your job, and don't want to lose it. Maybe it's better to be like Miguel and not ask too many questions.

68

THE END

To follow another path, turn to page 11.
To read the conclusion, turn to page 101.

You agree to the deal. A few days later, you hear from Carla. "You'll lose your job, of course, and your clearance," she says. "And you have to pay a fine."

As you and Carla prepare to meet the U.S. officials, you can't believe what's happened. You just wanted to help your country, first by finding terrorists, and then by telling the truth. Now you're lucky you're not going to jail.

THE END

To follow another path, turn to page 11.
To read the conclusion, turn to page 101.

You want to show everyone that the information you gave wasn't secret. You're a whistle-blower, not a criminal.

You wait months as government officials try to build evidence against you. They don't claim that you shared classified information. Instead they say you took information that may have been classified. Carla contacts the media to explain your case. The government is trying to make an example of you. It doesn't want other people to reveal everything about the work the NSA does.

Privacy advocates protest outside the NSA facility in Bluffdale, Utah, on July 4, 2013.

Thanks to Carla, more people learn about your case. Just before your trial, the U.S. Department of Justice makes a deal with you. It will drop the espionage charge if you plead guilty to a lesser charge of using a computer improperly. You won't have to spend any time in jail. You agree to the deal. Then you begin to tour the country. You speak out against the government seeking to arrest whistle-blowers like you. Some people support you, and some don't. But you know in your heart that you did the right thing.

THE END

To follow another path, turn to page 11.
To read the conclusion, turn to page 101.

"You're probably right," you tell Miguel. "I should just do my job."

You help run the computers that collect information from all over the country. The government has a list of people it considers suspicious. Software looks for certain words in their e-mail messages, in case they might be planning terrorist attacks. But you realize that many people on the list are probably not terrorists. And they don't know their personal information is being gathered.

You also read about a lawsuit that a private
organization filed against the U.S. government. It wants to stop the NSA from collecting information from innocent Americans. In the past the government worked with phone companies to get some of the information.

The government has been fighting the lawsuit for years. It says the legal battle might force the government to reveal state secrets.

You know some former NSA workers have stepped forward to help fight the government. They believe that spying on innocent Americans is wrong. The longer you work at the data center, the more you agree. You decide to quit your job at the NSA. You'll use your computer skills at a private company. Or maybe you'll join a group that works to protect Americans' right to privacy.

THE END

To follow another path, turn to page 11.
To read the conclusion, turn to page 101.

Social media is a great way to promote a cause you believe in or a group you are a member of.

CHAPTER 4

Social Media Goes to School

You've always been concerned about the earth. You join a group of kids at school who want to promote recycling. You call your club the Green Team. Your goal is to increase recycling both at school and in your town.

"Getting the word out in school is easy," says Molly, the club's president. "But if we want the whole town involved, we have to work harder."

75

"Why don't we use social media?" you say. "We can have a blog too. I can set it all up."

You go home and start working on a blog site and the accounts for other social media.

Turn the page.

When the club meets again, you show everyone what you've done.

"That looks great," Molly says.

"I could do better," a boy says. It's John, a friend of Molly's. He's new to the club.

"At my old school, I built websites all the time," John brags. "And I can take great pictures to post on the sites."

"Maybe we should let John have a shot," Molly says. The other members nod. Molly looks at you. "What do you think? Can we let John be in charge of social media?"

You heart sinks. You know you're good with social media. Maybe you should just quit the club if everyone thinks John can do a better job.

To stay in the Green Team, go to page **77**.
To leave the Green Team, turn to page **81**.

"OK," you say. "Let John do it. And I can help, if you need it."

"Oh, I won't need any help," John says.

A few days later, John shows everyone the sites he's created. They look pretty good. But you're not sure they're any better than what you did.

On Saturday Molly invites the group over to her house for a party. At the party you talk with some of the other kids about the teachers at school.

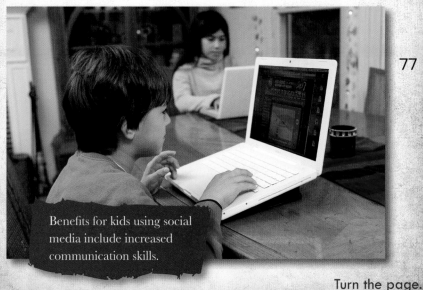

Benefits for kids using social media include increased communication skills.

Turn the page.

"Mrs. Green is just so fat," Rebecca says, and some kids laugh. Then other kids throw out names of other teachers. They make fun of them for having bad breath, being bald, or wearing ugly clothes.

"Hey guys, that's not very nice," Molly says as she hears some of the gossip. "What if those teachers found out what you said about them?"

"Oh, come on," Todd says. "Kids everywhere talk about their teachers. And there's no way anyone outside the group will find out."

The talk goes on for a little while before everyone switches to other topics. You notice John is sitting alone and not joining the conversation. Just as well. You don't have much to say to him.

When you get to school on Monday, you see Molly. She looks upset.

"Look at this," she says. She takes you outside. Other club members are crowded around a laptop. They're looking at a Facebook page called "Teacher Confessions."

"It's a confession page," Todd says. "It's looking for students in town to post things about their teachers. And to get it started, it has this." Todd clicks on a link. You hear a recording of voices—including yours!

"It's from the party," Molly says. "Someone was recording us, probably with a smart phone. And then the person started this page."

Turn the page.

Many cell phones today contain
recording devices built in.

You've heard about confession pages. Some
kids use them to rate other students' looks or
make fun of them. Usually the pages get shut
down pretty fast.

"Who would do this?" Rebecca asks.

"John had his phone out a lot," you say.

"Somebody has to say something to him,"
Molly says. "I think a big guy should do it." She
looks at you. You are the biggest kid in the group.

To confront John, turn to page **84.**

To say no, turn to page **85.**

"I think I'm going to look for another club," you tell Molly. "But I'll still come to club events."

You look at the social media pages John created for the Green Team. They aren't any better than what you could do. While you're on Facebook, you see a new page for your friend Maria. It has pictures of her, but they've been changed so she looks bald and fat. And the posts all say mean things about her.

The next day in school, you talk to Maria at lunchtime. She's crying.

Cyberbullying is a serious problem that can affect many people.

Turn the page.

"I don't know why someone would cyberbully you," you say.

"I don't know either," she says. "But the principal can't do anything unless someone did it using a school computer. My parents even called the police. They said it's not a crime to put up a fake social media page."

Todd, a friend from the Green Team, comes over.

"I think John did it," he says. "He was talking about how funny fake pages are."

82   "Somebody should stop him," Maria says, wiping the tears from her eyes.

"But we can't prove he did it," you say.

"You can," Todd says. "I'll bet you could hack into his computer and find out what he's posting."

You know there are many software programs that could help you get into John's computer. You also know it's illegal, but what he's done to Maria is so wrong.

83

Keep your social media passwords safe. People can hack into your accounts if they know your password.

To try to hack John's computer, turn to page **96.**

To not hack his computer, turn to page **98.**

You spot John outside. "We saw your new page on Facebook," you say.

"What are you talking about?" John asks.

"The confession page. You recorded us and put what we said about the teachers online."

"Prove it," John says.

You say that even without proof, you'll tell the principal and his parents.

"OK, I put up that page," John admits. "But it's no big deal."

84

"Look," John says. "If you don't tell anyone, I'll let you take over all the social media sites again."

You really want to be in charge of the Green Team social media again. But letting John get away with setting up the page seems wrong.

To not tell on John, turn to page **86.**

To tell on him, turn to page **89.**

"I don't want to get into anything with John," you say. "Including a fight."

Molly agrees. She decides that the group should tell Mrs. Perretta, the principal, about the confession page. A few kids go with her, but Todd stays behind.

"There's a way to get back at John without saying anything to him," Todd says. "You could set up a Facebook page about him."

"You mean like cyberbullying?"

Todd nods. "I'll help you," he says.

You know it would be easy to set up a fake social media account in John's name. But you're not sure it's the right thing to do.

To set up the page about John, turn to page **91**.

To tell Todd no, turn to page **94**.

"All right," you say. "I won't tell. And before the next meeting, tell Molly you have too much to do to keep up the social media sites."

John agrees. Meanwhile you tell Molly that John says he didn't create the confession page. You say, "Maybe he recorded the stuff just for fun and gave it to someone else. If he did, that page wasn't even started by someone in the club."

You're lying to a good friend, and it feels bad. But you can't tell Molly that you and John made a deal.

At the next meeting, Molly says that John has left the Green Team. Molly asks if you want to take over the social media pages. You agree.

You show the team some things you've been working on. Everybody says the material looks great.

Later that day you run into Todd. "That confession page is still up," he tells you. "More kids are posting things about the teachers."

"That's too bad," you say as you walk away. You hate lying to your friends.

The next day, Molly tells you that Mrs. Perretta, the school principal, has seen the page.

A simple comment online may seem harmless, but you don't know how your comments can impact others.

Turn the page.

"So she'll try to shut it down?" you ask.

"I think so," Molly says. "But she's going to shut down the Green Team and all the other school clubs!"

Molly explains that Mrs. Perretta will keep the clubs closed until the person who started the confession page comes forward. You can barely look at Molly. You realize you should have told the truth from the beginning. That was more important than being in charge of the social media sites.

THE END

To follow another path, turn to page 11.
To read the conclusion, turn to page 101.

"I can't do that, John," you say. "What you did was wrong."

"So you're going to tell on me," he says.

"I want to make sure that page comes down." You turn away. Out of the corner of your eye, you see John make a fist. You turn back, and he takes a swing at you. You duck, and he misses. You take a step toward him and push him away.

"Don't add to your troubles by fighting," you say. You go to Mrs. Perretta, the principal. You show her John's confession page.

Turn the page.

She shakes her head and frowns. "That's against the rule for use of social media, even if he created the page away from school. We'll make sure he's punished. Thanks for telling me."

You leave Mrs. Perretta's office knowing you did the right thing. And you have a feeling John won't stay on the Green Team. Maybe you'll be in charge of the social media sites again after all.

THE END

To follow another path, turn to page 11.
To read the conclusion, turn to page 101.

Over the next few days at school, you and Todd use your smart phones to secretly take pictures of John. Then you load them into your computer and change them. The software lets you twist and distort John's face and body. You show Todd the new pictures. "This is going to be great!" Todd grins.

The fake page is up the next day. Kids all over school quickly know about it—including John. One morning, he comes up to you before class.

"I know you put up that page about me," John says. "And you're going to pay for it."

The next day you get a message that Mrs. Perretta wants to see you.

Your stomach churns as you enter her office. John is sitting there too.

On Mrs. Perretta's computer is the fake page you created.

Mrs. Perretta looks at you sternly. "Are you involved with creating this page?"

You nod.

"Did you do any of the work on it here in school?"

Tell a teacher or parent about any cyberbullying at your school instead of getting back at the bully.

"No," you say.

"What about those pictures?" John says. "I can tell you took them here."

"Is that right?" Mrs. Perretta asks.

You nod again.

"You know our rules," the principal says. "Any cyberbullying done on school property means a suspension. Did anyone help you with this?"

You think about Todd. This time it seems OK to lie to protect him. "No."

You sink deep in your chair as Mrs. Perretta calls your parents. They won't like the idea of you being suspended. You know it will be a long time before they let you use the computer again.

THE END

To follow another path, turn to page 11.
To read the conclusion, turn to page 101.

"I won't do it, Todd," you say. "Just because John is a jerk doesn't mean we should do something mean to him."

The next day Molly tells you that the principal can't do anything about the confession page unless John created it during school time.

"Maybe I should have said something to him before," you say to Molly.

"You still can," she says. "I'll go with you."

At the end of the day, the two of you wait for John to leave school. He sees you and stops.

"Did I miss a Green Team meeting?" he asks Molly.

"This isn't about the team," she says. "This is about your confession page. Take it down."

John tries to hold back a smile. "Confession page? Oh, yeah, I heard about that. Wonder who would do something like that?"

You take a step toward John. "You would. And we want you to take it down."

You hear the anger in your voice as you get in John's face. You've never liked John. You think that in this moment, you'll punch him if he says no. But you see the look in his eyes—he's afraid of you.

"All right, I'll take it down," he says. "It was just a joke."

"We didn't think it was very funny," Molly says.

That night you see the confession page is gone. You didn't like threatening John, but at least it was for a good reason.

THE END

To follow another path, turn to page 11.
To read the conclusion, turn to page 101.

Todd calls you that night. "I saw John working on his computer in the library," Todd says. "He typed his password into a Facebook account. It's his last name spelled backwards and the numbers 0412."

"Probably his birthday," you say. "Let's see what I can do."

You hang up and get to work. You don't know John's username, but you try different forms of his name along with the password. After a few minutes, you get it! You see all his information. Then you look for the page you believe he created to bully Maria. You use her name for the login and the same password—and it works! You call Todd and tell him you've caught John.

You tell your parents about the page, and John's role in creating it.

Your parents call Maria's parents. The next day, you see Maria in school.

"My parents called the principal this morning," she says. "There's nothing the school can do unless we can prove John created the page in school."

In some instances, cyberbullying is a crime and should be reported to law enforcement.

"So he can get away with cyberbullying?" you ask.

"No," Maria says. "We're going to take him and his parents to court. Maybe that will get him to take down the page."

97

You're glad that you were able to help Maria. And you hope that John gets the punishment he deserves.

THE END

To follow another path, turn to page 11.
To read the conclusion, turn to page 101.

"I'd like to help, Maria," you say. "But I don't want to get into trouble for hacking."

Over the next week, you hear kids talking about the page. More mean posts appear about Maria. You tell your parents you think John is responsible, but you have no proof. One day you realize you haven't seen Maria in school for a few days. You ask Todd about her. His face grows serious.

"You didn't hear? She's in the hospital."

"What happened?" you ask.

Todd explains that someone using a fake name posted on Maria's own page, saying how ugly she was. "The person wrote, 'The world would be a better place if you weren't in it.' And then Maria tried to kill herself."

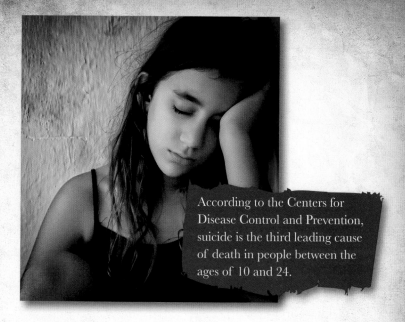

According to the Centers for Disease Control and Prevention, suicide is the third leading cause of death in people between the ages of 10 and 24.

You stare at Todd, horrified. "Is she OK?" you ask.

"She will be. But her family is moving away."

You feel awful. You wish you had done more to help. You decide your school needs a new club—one meant to prevent cyberbullying. And you're going to start it.

THE END

To follow another path, turn to page 11.
To read the conclusion, turn to page 101.

The tablet computer was invented in 2010 and now has a place in many homes. What will be the next technological advancement to help promote social media?

CHAPTER 5

The Social Media Explosion

Social media sites have become a form of instant communication all over the world. With software and technology changing so quickly, no one knows what the next big social networking site will be or how it will be used. But some issues are likely to remain important for years to come.

Governments' interests in tracking what people say and do online have raised concerns about privacy. Should users expect private tweets or e-mails to remain private? Or is a government's duty to protect its citizens more important? Even if a government doesn't use social media to spy on citizens, companies can track people's habits through their social media use.

101

Turn the page.

This issue made headlines in June 2013. Edward Snowden worked for a company that provided computer services to the National Security Agency. He gave information about the NSA's surveillance of American citizens' cell phone calls and e-mails to the press. Many people were outraged at the invasion of privacy. Others supported the government's actions. Snowden fled the United States to avoid being arrested for leaking the information to the press.

And the issue of cyberbullying raises questions and concerns too. When does a student's right to say something mean about other students or teachers deserve protection under the First Amendment?

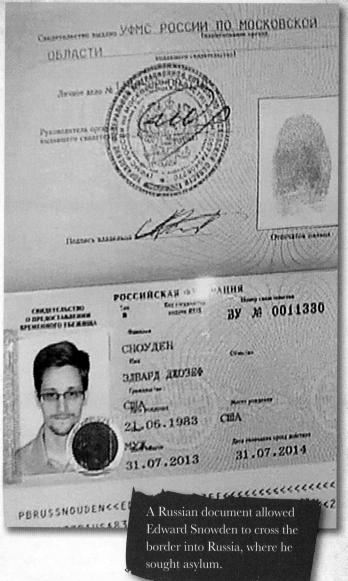

A Russian document allowed Edward Snowden to cross the border into Russia, where he sought asylum.

Because laws are different in every country, users may post a message in the U.S. but find they've broken the law in another country. Or more likely, the company that allowed the message to be posted could face legal trouble.

Trying to predict the future for social media isn't easy. Some experts say people might lose interest in reading about their friends' lives. On the other hand, social media could be used to link technology like never before. An electronics company could build a system into all its products that would allow them to interact.

For example, you could use your phone at school to check what's inside the refrigerator at home.

No one knows exactly what social media will be able to do years from now. But it promises to remain a large part of how we share ideas and stay in touch with others.

Social media is constantly growing, as technology creates easier ways for people to interact with each other.

TIMELINE

1969—The U.S. government links computers at four universities, creating ARPANET.

1971—ARPANET users begin exchanging e-mails.

1970s—The first personal computers are produced.

1981—IBM launches its personal computer (PC).

1984—Apple produces its personal computer, the MacIntosh.

1985—Computer company Symbolics registers the first Internet domain name, symbolics.com.

1989—Swiss software designer Tim Berners-Lee develops the World Wide Web.

1993—Mosaic and other web browsers allow easy access to the Internet from personal computers.

1995—The number of Web users around the world reaches 16 million.

2002—Friendster is launched.

2003—MySpace is founded.

2004—Mark Zuckerberg starts thefacebook, which later becomes Facebook.

2005—The number of Internet users is more than 1 billion.

2006—Twitter is launched.

2012—Facebook has 1 billion users.

2013—A post on a hacked Twitter account falsely reports that the White House has been attacked by terrorists; the NSA's Utah Data Center opens; NSA contract employee Edward Snowden leaks top-secret information to the press about the extent of the U.S. government's surveillance of the social media and phone use of Americans.

OTHER PATHS TO EXPLORE

In this book you've explored major issues involved in the creation of the social network. Perspectives on history are as varied as the people who lived it. Seeing history from many points of view is an important part of understanding it. Here are ideas for other points of view to explore.

You work for a social media company in a country with strict laws against free speech. Someone posts a message that is offensive. The country's government asks you to take it down. Would you remove the post or defend the user's right to free speech? (Common Core: Integration of Knowledge and Ideas)

An official at the company you work for posts online comments that upset some customers. Using ideas from the text, explain what you might do to help restore your company's reputation.
(Common Core: Key Ideas and Details)

You're a business owner considering software that can block access to social media sites at work. What are some of the reasons why you might do this? On the other hand, what are some ways that social media sites might help your business?
(Common Core: Integration of Knowledge and Ideas)

READ MORE

Berlatsky, Noah, ed. *Social Networking.* Detroit: Greenhaven Press, 2013.

Hasday, Judy L. *Facebook and Mark Zuckerberg.* Greensboro, N.C.: Morgan Reynolds Pub., 2012.

Stuckey, Rachel. *Cyber Bullying.* New York: Crabtree Publishing Company, 2013.

Yomtov, Nel. *Internet Inventors.* New York: Children's Press, 2013.

INTERNET SITES

Use FactHound fun way to find Internet sites related to this book. All of the sites on FactHound have been researched by our staff.

Here's all you do:
Visit *www.facthound.com*
Type in this code: 9781476541884

GLOSSARY

analyst (EH-nuh-luhst)—a person who reviews data for certain information

classified document (KLAH-suh-fide DAHK-yuh-muhnt)—sensitive information that could cause damage to national security if released

clearance (KLIHR-uhnss)—permission to do something or have access to certain information

cyberbullying (SY-buhr-buh-lee-ing)—using social media to attack or make fun of others

cyberwarfare (SY-buhr-wor-fayr)—attacks carried out on a country or group using computers

dean (DEEN)—an official at a college

encryption (in-KRIP-shuhn)—a system used to make computer information secure

investor (in-VEST-uhr)—a person who provides money for a project or business in return for a share of the profits

media (MEE-dee-uh)—TV, radio, newspapers, Internet, and other communication forms that send messages to large groups of people

network (NET-wurk)—a system of things that are connected to each other

simulation (sim-yuh-LAY-shuhn)—a copy or imitation of a real-life situation

stock (STOK)—the value of a company, divided into shares when sold to investors

surveillance (suhr-VAY-luhnss)—the act of keeping very close watch on someone, someplace, or something

terrorist (TER-uhr-ist)—a person who commits or threatens to commit violent acts to try to achieve a political goal

warrant (WOR-uhnt)—a legal document that allows law enforcement officials to collect information

BIBLIOGRAPHY

Bamford, James. "The NSA Is Building the Country's Biggest Spy Center (Watch What You Say)." *Wired*. 15 March 2012. 30 Sept. 2013. http://www.wired.com/threatlevel/2012/03/ff_nsadatacenter

Carr, Jeffrey. *Inside Cyber Warfare*. Sebastopol, Calif.: O'Reilly, 2012.

Chow, Andrew. "Teen Sues Classmates Over Facebook Cyberbullying." *Findlaw*. 2 May 2012. 30 Sept. 2013. http://blogs.findlaw.com/law_and_life/2012/05/teen-sued-classmates-over-facebook-cyberbullying.html

Computer History Museum—Internet History. 30 Sept. 2013. www.computerhistory.org/internet_history

DARPA History. 30 Sept. 2013. www.darpa.mil/about/history/history.aspx

Gragido, Will, and John Pirc. *Cybercrime and Espionage: An Analysis of Subversive Multivector Threats*. Rockland, Mass.: Syngress, 2011.

Kirkpatrick, David. *The Facebook Effect: The Inside Story of the Company That Is Connecting the World*. New York: Simon and Schuster, 2010.

Mayer, Jane. "The Secret Sharer: Is Thomas Drake an Enemy of the State?" *The New Yorker*. 23 May 2011. 30 Sept. 2013. http://www.newyorker.com/reporting/2011/05/23/110523fa_fact_mayer

National Security Agency/Central Security Service. 30 Sept. 2013. www.nsa.gov

Van Dijck, José. *The Culture of Connectivity: A Critical History of Social Media*. New York: Oxford University Press, 2013.

World Wide Web Foundation—History of the Web. 30 Sept. 2013. http://www.webfoundation.org/vision/history-of-the-web/

INDEX